Petie the Pitbull

By Erika Wiseman

AuthorHouse™
1663 Liberty Drive
Bloomington, IN 47403
www.authorhouse.com
Phone: 833-262-8899

Because of the dynamic nature of the Internet, any web addresses or links contained in this book may have changed
since publication and may no longer be valid. The views expressed in this work are solely those of the author and do not
necessarily reflect the views of the publisher, and the publisher hereby disclaims any responsibility for them.

Any people depicted in stock imagery provided by Thinkstock are models,
and such images are being used for illustrative purposes only.
Certain stock imagery © Thinkstock.

This book is printed on acid-free paper.

ISBN: 978-1-4918-9925-0 (sc)
ISBN: 978-1-4918-9926-7 (e)

Print information available on the last page.

Published by AuthorHouse 08/18/2022

authorHOUSE®

I
was
Born
on August 8th
2010
Same as my mommy, For
i was her
B-day
present.

When Lucas comes to visit, beulah goes crazy with excitment ✳

Lucas + Dad

Dad loves me too! We play peek-a-boo with the bed covers!

3

Lucas is my human Brother

My human sister's name is Emma

Steve is my Dad

Sally
is my sister who lives
in Florida. Eight hours
From
me!

These are the two sisters
i live with now. It took a
few weeks to get use to me,
but now we play all the time!
The red one is LucyLou and
the blonde one is beulah.
Beulah already has a book out,
so she thought i should do a
book too.

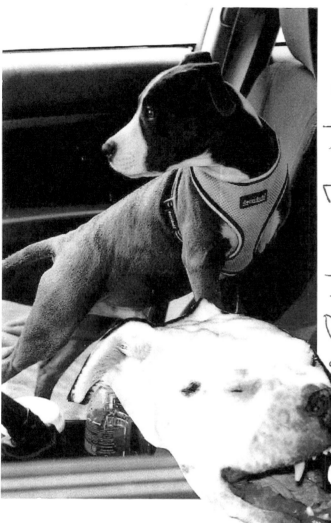

Every day, unless mom's cooking, I get to go for rides and walks at the park. I love the woods. Mother Nature is so beautiful.

Since we play a bunch with our mouths mom makes sure that all of our teeth are clean. She thinks we look a little scary when we play.

Beulah, Lucylou, and myself nap together. I love to snuggle up to them! Beulah snores the loudest.

Mom takes
us Almost
Everywhere
she goes
thats
Awesome

All this in my Backyard.

I stay busy!

14

Even though
Sassy is a lizard,
we are also Friends
Forever!

Sassy
loves
to
Climb
trees,
and sitting
on my
head

she eats crickets
t sometimes
chicken.
Even ham

My Mom loves winter the most. Dad prefers the summer.

← We are eating the snow. Lucylou said not to eat it if it's yellow!

First Snow!
For me

Fun
Fun
Fun!

The
Snow is so
Fabulous!

After the snow melted
Lucy lou got awfully sick.
She lived twelve human
years and we will all miss
her so very much!

Although i know she
is just over the rainbows, it
will take lots of time not to
be sad anymore. I sure am
glad i got to meet her, love
her, and play with her while
she was here.
I MISS YOU Lucy! Lou

Lucy
Lou

Mom Say's Lucy lou would
want us to Keep having
Fun!

Beulah
Missing lucy

I Love
playing with
the
Broom

Next Couple pages are
some pictures of me
being silly with all
of my
Friends from the dog park.
We run and run until i
sniff something for awhile.
IF i am lucky there will
be some mudd puddles!

My friends are Very
Colorful + Fun + Full of
energy because our parents
make us take a nap, and
drink lots of water
H_2O

unfortunately, some people are afraid to pet or play with me, cause i am a pitbull. I wish humans knew that if you love us we will love you. IF you treat us real bad, that is how we will act. It's like we are permanently little kids, so be nice + caring then we shall be too! only bad people have bad dogs.

Can You Find me Twice

I have to Finish so i can take a nap with my sister, beulah.

Always give love and kindness to absolutely everyone!

Petie's Paws

Look For Beulah's

Second book

Coming Soon!

Printed in the United States
by Baker & Taylor Publisher Services